ICE CREAMS
AND
SORBETS

TIGER BOOKS INTERNATIONAL
LONDON

Introduction

Desserts have long been adored as the perfect ending to a meal, and with today's move towards a lighter, healthier style of eating, ice creams and sorbets have become increasingly popular.

Ice cream has always been a great favourite with both children and adults. It is light and refreshing and has a wonderfully creamy texture. Ice cream can be made in a great variety of flavours, from old favourites such as strawberry and chocolate, to new and exciting ones such as honey and pine nut or cashew. Ice creams are also perfect for utilising whatever fruit is in season. Although most ice creams actually contain cream, if you want a healthy alternative you can use yogurt and there are a few recipes in this book which do this. And if you wish to make your ice cream a little more impressive, why not combine it with sponge or a biscuit base, for example.

Sorbets, too, have shown a great rise in popularity. They are now served regularly as a dessert, as well as in their more traditional role as a refresher between courses. Sorbets have become so popular because they are simple to prepare, use few ingredients and have none of the fat of more traditional desserts. Sorbets are not limited to everyday fruit such as lemon, you can use almost any fruit which is in season. We have included a recipe for Guava Mint Sorbet and Coconut Sorbet as well as the more familiar ones such as strawberry and orange.

So if you want to satisfy your sweet tooth, but not be too self-indulgent, why not try an ice cream or sorbet – you can make it as simple or as exotic as you wish.

3288
This edition published in 1993 by Tiger Books International PLC, London
© 1993 Coombe Books
Printed and bound in Singapore
All rights reserved
ISBN 1 85501 310 X

COFFEE AND RAISIN ICE CREAM

Perfect for a sweet finale or just as a treat

MAKES 20fl.oz/1 pint

280ml/½ pint full cream milk
100g/4oz sugar
6 tsps coffee granules or powder
1 tsp cocoa powder
1 egg yolk
1 tsp vanilla essence
280ml/½ pint whipping or double cream
50g/2oz raisins

1. Heat the milk and sugar until almost boiling.

2. Add the coffee and cocoa, stir and leave to cool.

3. Beat the egg yolk with the vanilla essence until frothy.

4. Whip the cream until stiff.

5. Pour the cream and coffee mixture into the egg mixture and stir well.

6. Add the raisins and stir again.

7. Freeze until firm (3-4 hours), stirring several times during freezing.

8. Defrost for 10-15 minutes before serving.

TIME: Preparation takes 3-4 hours, including freezing.

SERVING IDEA: Serve with home-made cookies.

VARIATION: For a chocolate flavour use light carob powder in place of coffee.

STRAWBERRY ICE CREAM

*This ice cream can be made with the pieces of fruit left in
small chunks, or mixed smooth with a hand mixer.*

SERVES 4

250ml/8fl oz egg custard (see Banana
   Ice Cream recipe)
60ml/2fl oz single cream
150g/5oz strawberries, washed and hulled

1. Either chop the strawberries into small pieces and mix them into the egg custard, or add them whole to the custard and blend until smooth with a hand mixer.

2. Stir in the cream and pour into the bowl of an ice cream maker. Set the machine in motion. *

3. When the ice cream has 'taken', spoon into a container and keep in the freezer until needed.

* If an ice cream maker is not available, part freeze the mixture in a bowl, whisk and refreeze. Whisk again, pour into a covered container and freeze until firm.

TIME: If you already have some egg custard the preparation takes 5 minutes and freezing time is 45 minutes to 1 hour using the ice cream maker method. If you have to make the custard, an extra 30 minutes will be needed.

SERVING IDEA: Serve with whole strawberries or with a coulis of fresh strawberries and a little sugar.

VARIATION: The mixture may be sieved after Step 1 if you wish to remove the strawberry seeds.

HONEY ICE CREAM WITH PINE KERNEL NUTS

*This ice cream, with its flavour of honey and pine nuts, is
so good you'll find yourself making it regularly.*

SERVES 4

30ml/2 tbsps honey
6 egg yolks
500ml/18fl oz milk
30g/2 tbsps pine nuts

1. Whisk the honey and the egg yolks together for 1 minute.

2. Bring the milk to the boil.

3. Pour the milk over the egg mixture, whisking continuously.

4. Pour this mixture back into the saucepan, add the pine nuts and place over a very low heat, stirring continuously, until the sauce thickens and will coat the back of a spoon.

5. Allow the mixture to cool and then pour into the bowl of an ice cream maker. Set the machine in motion. *

6. Once the ice cream has 'taken', spoon into a container and keep in the freezer until needed.

* If an ice cream maker is not available, part freeze the mixture in a bowl, whisk until smooth then refreeze. Whisk again and freeze in a covered container until firm.

TIME: Preparation time is approximately 25 minutes and freezing time is between 45 minutes and 1 hour – longer if prepared without an ice cream maker.

VARIATION: Try a variety of different honeys in this ice cream.

WATCHPOINT: Whisk briskly as you pour the milk onto the egg mixture, as the eggs can coagulate quickly with the absence of sugar in this recipe.

CASSATA

This Italian ice cream is rich, creamy and justly famous.

SERVES 6-8

Almond Layer
2 eggs, separated
60g/2oz icing sugar
140ml/¼ pint double cream
2.5ml/½ tsp almond essence

Chocolate Layer
2 eggs, separated
60g/2oz icing sugar
140ml/¼ pint double cream
60g/2oz plain chocolate
30g/2 tbsps cocoa
25ml/1½ tbsps water

Fruit Layer
280ml/½ pint double cream
30ml/2 tbsps maraschino or light rum
1 egg white
60g/2oz icing sugar
60g/2oz mixed glacé fruit
30g/1oz shelled chopped pistachios

1. To prepare the almond layer, beat egg whites until stiff peaks form, gradually beating in the icing sugar, a spoonful at a time. Lightly beat the egg yolks and fold in the whites. Whip the cream with the almond essence until soft peaks form and fold into the egg mixture. Lightly oil a 20cm/8-inch round cake tin. Pour in the almond layer mixture and smooth over the top. Cover with cling film and freeze until firm.

2. To prepare the chocolate layer, beat the egg whites until stiff but not dry and gradually beat in the icing sugar. Whip the cream until soft and fold into the egg white mixture. Put the chocolate in the top of a double boiler over simmering water. Remove it from the heat and stir in the egg yolks. Combine cocoa and water and add to the chocolate mixture. Allow to cool and then fold into the egg white mixture. Spoon the chocolate layer over the almond layer and return, covered, to the freezer.

3. To make the fruit layer, whip the cream until soft peaks form. Whip the egg white until about the same consistency as cream. Gradually add the icing sugar, beating well after each addition. Combine the two mixtures, fold in the rum, fruit and nuts. Spread this mixture on top of the chocolate layer, cover and freeze until firm.

4. To serve, loosen the cassata from around the edges of the pan with a small knife. Place a hot cloth around the pan for a few seconds to help loosen. Turn out onto a serving plate and cut into wedges to serve.

TIME: Preparation can take several hours, so that one ice cream layer can freeze before another is added.

SERVING IDEAS: Sprinkle the top layer of the cassata with more chopped pistachios and chocolate curls. Decorate with rosettes of whipped cream, if desired.

Frozen Meringue Cream

This is a richer version of a typical iced milk dessert found all over Spain.

MAKES 1150ml/2 pints

1150ml/2 pints single cream
90g/3oz sugar
1 whole vanilla pod
60ml/4 tbsps brandy
2 egg whites

1. Combine the cream, sugar and vanilla pod in a deep, heavy-based saucepan.

2. Cook over very gentle heat for about 10 minutes, stirring frequently to dissolve the sugar. Do not allow the cream to boil.

3. Switch off heat, cover the pan and leave to infuse for about 15 minutes. Strain into a bowl to remove the vanilla pod and set aside to cool completely.

4. Beat the egg whites until stiff but not dry.

5. Fold them into the cooled cream mixture. Add brandy and chill completely.

6. Pour into a shallow pan or ice cube tray and freeze until slushy.

7. Spoon the mixture into a food processor and work until smoth. Alternatively, use an electric mixer. Return the mixture to the freezer and freeze until nearly solid. Repeat the mixing procedure and then freeze in a rigid plastic container until firm. Allow the container to stand at room temperature for about 10 minutes before serving.

TIME: Preparation takes about 20 minutes. Allow at least 2 hours for the freezing and mixing procedure.

SERVING IDEAS: Serve with chocolate sauce, fruit sauce or fresh fruit, biscuits, or simply sprinkled with ground cinnamon or nutmeg.

PREPARATION: The freezing and mixing procedure eliminates large ice crystals from the sorbet. If desired, the sorbet may be processed again just before serving, but this will result in a very soft mixture.

Chocolate Chip Ice Cream

An ideal treat for chocolate lovers everywhere!

SERVES 8

200g/7oz chocolate, chopped or grated
250ml/9fl oz milk
3 eggs yolks
90g/3oz sugar
250ml/9fl oz double cream, lightly
  whipped
150g/5oz finely chopped chocolate

---

1. Stir the chopped or grated chocolate into the milk in a small, heavy-based saucepan and stir over a gentle heat until the chocolate melts.

2. Put the egg yolks into a bowl with the sugar and beat until thick and creamy. Add the chocolate milk and beat. Return the chocolate mixture to the saucepan and stir continuously over a moderate heat until the mixture is thick and will coat the back of a spoon.

3. Strain the chocolate custard into a bowl and cool in the refrigerator. When quite cold, fold in the whipped double cream.

4. Pour into ice trays and freeze until the mixture begins to set around the edges. Pour into a bowl and beat. Stir in the chopped chocolate. Return the ice cream to the ice trays and freeze for 30 minutes.

5. Repeat the beating and freezing method every 30 minutes, until the ice cream is really thick. Freeze until firm.

TIME: Preparation takes 30 minutes, plus freezing time and cooking takes 6-8 minutes.

LOW-FAT BROWN BREAD ICE CREAM

This ice-cream is ideal for slimmers.

SERVES 4

45g/1½ oz brown breadcrumbs
45g/1½ oz brown sugar
3 eggs, separated
280ml/½ pint Greek yogurt
1 tbsp honey (optional)

1. Place the breadcrumbs on a baking tray and cover with the sugar.

2. Place in a moderately hot oven 190°C/ 375°F/Gas Mark 5 for 20 minutes or until they begin to brown and caramelise. Stir once or twice so they brown evenly. Leave aside.

3. Beat the egg whites until stiff.

4. In a separate bowl, mix the egg yolks into the yogurt and then fold in the egg whites. Add the honey if desired and fold in evenly.

5. Add the cold breadcrumbs and mix well.

6. Place in the freezer, and when setting point is reached, stir the sides to prevent ice crystals forming.

7. Return to the freezer and leave until set.

TIME: Preparation takes 20 minutes, cooking and freezing takes 20 minutes plus 4-5 hours or overnight.

COOK'S TIP: Remove from the freezer and place in the refrigerator about ¾ of an hour before serving.

VARIATION: Maple syrup may be used in place of honey.

GUAVA MINT SORBET

The exotic taste of guava works well with mint in this delicious sorbet.

MAKES 850ml/1½ pints

180g/6oz granulated sugar
280ml/1½ pints water
4 ripe guavas
30g/2 tbsps chopped fresh mint
1 lime
1 egg white
Fresh mint leaves for garnish

1. Combine the sugar and water in a heavy-based saucepan and bring slowly to the boil to dissolve the sugar. When the mixture is a clear syrup, boil rapidly for 30 seconds. Allow to cool to room temperature and then chill in the refrigerator.

2. Cut the guavas in half and scoop out the pulp. Discard the peels and seeds and purée the fruit until smooth in a food processor. Add the mint and combine with cold syrup. Add lime juice until the right balance of sweetness is reached.

3. Pour the mixture into a shallow container and freeze until slushy. Process again to break up ice crystals and then freeze until firm.

4. Whip the egg white until stiff but not dry. Process the sorbet again and when smooth, add the egg white. Mix once or twice and then freeze again until firm.

5. Remove from the freezer 15 minutes before serving and keep in the refrigerator.

6. Garnish each serving with mint leaves.

TIME: Preparation takes about 3 hours, plus freezing.

BLACK BOTTOM ICE CREAM PIE

*Unbelievably simple, yet incredibly delicious and impressive,
this pie is a perfect ending to a summer meal or a spicy one anytime.*

MAKES 1 PIE

8-10 digestive biscuits, crushed
120g/4oz butter or margarine, melted
740g/1¼ pints coffee ice cream
60g/2oz plain chocolate, melted
120g/4oz dessicated coconut
Dark rum

1. Crush biscuits with a rolling pin or in a food processor. Mix with melted butter or margarine.

2. Press into an 8½ inch false-bottomed flan dish. Chill thoroughly in the refrigerator.

3. Meanwhile, combine 4 tbsps coconut with the melted chocolate. When cooled but not solidified, add about a quarter of the coffee ice cream, mixing well.

4. Spread the mixture on the base of the crust and freeze until firm.

5. Soften the remaining ice cream with an electric mixer or food processor and spread over the chocolate-coconut layer. Re-freeze until firm.

6. Toast the remaining coconut in a moderate oven, stirring frequently until pale golden brown. Allow to cool completely.

7. Remove the pie from the freezer and leave in the refrigerator 30 minutes before serving. Push up the base of the dish and place the pie on a serving plate. Sprinkle the top with toasted coconut. Cut into wedges and drizzle with rum before serving.

TIME: 25 minutes, plus freezing time.

VARIATION: If desired, use vanilla ice cream in place of the coffee.

FRUIT SORBETS

*Real fruit sorbets are a delicious way of finishing
off meals on hot summer evenings.*

SERVES 4-6

Orange Sorbet
225g/8oz sugar
250ml/9fl oz fresh orange juice
90ml/3fl oz fresh lemon juice
Zest of 1 orange

Pear Sorbet
5 tbsps sugar
450g/1lb pears, peeled and chopped
3 tbsps lemon juice
1 egg white and a pinch salt, whipped
   until stiff

Apple Sorbet
120g/4oz sugar
450g/1lb apples, peeled and chopped
2 tbsps lemon juice
1 egg white and a pinch of salt, beaten
   until stiff

ORANGE SORBET
1. Dissolve the sugar in 2 cups water,
bring to the boil and boil continuously for
10 minutes. Set aside to cool.

2. Blanch the orange zest in boiling water.

3. Mix the cooled syrup with the orange
and lemon juice, and stir in the zest. Pour
the mixture into a plastic container and
place in the freezer.

4. Remove the sorbet from the freezer
every 30 minutes and beat with a fork
until it has completely crystallized.

PEAR SORBET
1. Dissolve the sugar in 150ml/5fl oz
water, add the chopped pear, bring to the
boil and boil continuously for 10 minutes.
Set aside to cool.

2. Once cool, blend the above in a
blender until smooth. Stir in the lemon
juice.

3. Pour into a plastic container and freeze
for 1 hour.

4. After 1 hour, remove the sorbet and
beat it well with a fork. Incorporate the
beaten egg white gently, using a metal
spoon.

5. Cover and return to the freezer until
needed.

APPLE SORBET
1. Dissolve the sugar in 175ml/6fl oz
water, bring to the boil and boil
continuously for 5 minutes. Set aside to
cool.

2. Blend the cooled syrup, the apple and
the lemon juice in a blender until smooth.

3. Pour into a plastic container and freeze
for 1 hour.

4. After 1 hour, gently incorporate the egg
white using a wooden spoon. Return the
sorbet to the freezer until needed.

TIME: Preparation takes about 10 minutes, plus freezing time for each of the sorbets.

FREEZER TIP: Any of the sorbets can be made in advance and stored in the freezer.
Remove a few minutes before serving.

KULFI (INDIAN ICE CREAM)

Kulfi is by far the most popular ice cream in India. It is firmer than conventional ice cream and is usually set in small tin or aluminium moulds. You can, however, use either small yogurt pots or a plastic ice cream box.

SERVES 6-8

150ml/5fl oz fresh milk
2 tbsps ground rice
1 tbsp ground almonds
450ml/14½ oz tin evaporated milk
1 level tsp ground cardamom
50g/2oz sugar
450ml/15fl oz double cream
1 tbsp rosewater or 5-6 drops of any other
   flavouring such as vanilla, almond etc.
25g/1oz shelled, unsalted pistachio nuts,
   lightly crushed

1. Heat the milk until it is lukewarm.

2. Put the ground rice and ground almonds into a small bowl and gradually add the warm milk, a little at a time, and make a thin paste of pouring consistency. Stir continuously and break up any lumps. If any lumps remain, sieve the paste.

3. Heat evaporated milk to boiling point and add the ground cardamom.

4. Take the pan off the heat and gradually add the almond/rice mixture, stirring continuously.

5. Add the sugar and cream and place the pan over medium heat, cook the mixture for 12-15 minutes, stirring continuously. Remove the pan from heat and allow the mixture to cool slightly.

6. Add the rosewater flavouring and half of the pistachio nuts, stir and mix well. Allow the mixture to cool completely, stirring frequently to prevent a skin from forming on the surface.

7. When the mixture has cooled completely, put it into a plastic ice cream box or individual moulds.

8. Top with the remaining pistachio nuts and place in the freezer or in the ice-making compartment of a refrigerator for 4-5 hours.

9. Place the kulfi in the refrigerator for 1½ -1¾ hours before serving. This will soften the kulfi slightly and will make it easier to cut into desired size when it is set in an ice cream box. The time required to soften the kulfi will vary according to the size of the container used.

TIME: Preparation takes 10 minutes, cooking takes 15-20 minutes.

STRIPED SORBET

A tricoloured iced treat that can be prepared well ahead,
this is a wonderful way to end a summer meal.

SERVES 4

570ml/1 pint water
225g/8oz sugar
Juice of 1-2 lemons
8 kiwi fruit, peeled and roughly chopped
4 ripe bananas, peeled and
   roughly chopped
450g/1lb raspberries, fresh or well
   drained frozen
2 egg whites
1 banana
1 kiwi fruit, sliced and whole
   raspberries to garnish

1. Combine the water and sugar in a heavy-based saucepan. Bring slowly to the boil to dissolve the sugar.

2. When the sugar is completely dissolved, boil the syrup rapidly for about 1 minute. Allow it to cool completely and then refrigerate until completely cold.

3. Purée the kiwi fruit in a food processor, sieving to remove the seeds if desired. Purée the banana and the raspberries separately. Sieve the raspberries to remove the seeds.

4. Divide the cold syrup in 3 parts and mix each with one of the fruit purées. Taste each and add about 15-30ml/1-2 tbsps of lemon juice to each fruit syrup, depending on the sweetness of the fruit.

5. Freeze the fruit syrups separately until almost solid, about 2 hours, then mix again in the food processor to break up ice crystals. Freeze again separately until solid.

6. Whip the egg whites until stiff. Process the sorbets again, separately, dividing the egg white among all three.

7. Pour the raspberry sorbet into a bowl or mould and freeze until firm.

8. Pour the banana sorbet on top and freeze again.

9. Finish with the kiwi sorbet and freeze overnight or until firm.

10. To unmould, dip briefly in hot water and invert on a plate. Garnish with the prepared fruit.

TIME: Preparation takes about 35 minutes. The sorbets will take at least 2 hours to freeze before their first mixing. Once layered, the sorbets should be allowed to freeze overnight.

Prune Ice Cream

A simple-to-make, rich-tasting ice cream.

SERVES 4

250ml/8fl oz egg custard (see Banana
   Ice Cream recipe)
10 prunes, stoned
1 squeeze of lemon juice

1. Process the prunes with the lemon juice in a food processor. The prunes will form a thick dark paste.

2. Put this prune paste in a large bowl and pour over the egg custard.

3. Blend with a hand mixer until quite smooth.

4. Pour into the bowl of an ice cream maker and set the machine in motion. *

5. Once the ice cream has 'taken', spoon into a container and keep in the freezer until needed.

* If an ice cream maker is not available, part freeze the mixture in a bowl, whisk and refreeze. Whisk again, pour into a covered container and freeze until firm.

TIME: Preparation, if you already have the egg custard, will take about 8 minutes, and freezing time approximately 45 minutes to 1 hour using the ice cream maker – longer if preparing without an ice cream maker.

SERVING IDEA: Serve with prunes which have been marinaded in a fruit alcohol. Place small scoops of ice cream on the prunes and pour over the marinade.

COOK'S TIP: Ice cream should ideally be kept at -12°C/10°F, but as most freezers work a few degrees below this temperature, it is advisable to remove the ice cream from the freezer 10 minutes before serving.

STRAWBERRY SORBET

*Serve at the end of a very rich meal, or between the main
course and dessert, if serving a light summer dinner.*

SERVES 4

1 medium lemon
280ml/½ pint water
175g/6oz sugar
675g/1½ lbs strawberries
2 egg whites

1. Pare the lemon rind from the lemon and put into the water with the sugar.

2. Heat slowly until the sugar has dissolved then boil for 5 minutes.

3. Strain and set aside to cool.

4. Hull the strawberries, reserving a few for decoration. Press the remainder through a nylon sieve and add the juice of half the lemon.

5. Whisk the egg whites until very stiff.

6. Combine all the ingredients well.

7. Put into an airtight container and place in the freezer.

8. Remove when half frozen, beat well and return to the freezer until frozen.

9. Place in the refrigerator about 1 hour before serving.

10. Serve in wine glasses topped with the whole berries.

TIME: Preparation takes 20 minutes, cooking takes 5 minutes.
Freezing takes about 8 hours.

COOK'S TIP: It is better to leave the sorbet in the freezer overnight at the end of Step 8.

35

CARAMEL ICE CREAM

*A smooth ice cream with the flavour of toffee,
served with a creamy caramel sauce.*

SERVES 4

3 egg yolks
150g/5oz sugar
250ml/8 fl oz milk
30ml/2 tbsps double cream
150ml/5fl oz water

1. Whisk the egg yolks with 25g/1oz sugar until the mixture whitens.

2. Bring the milk to the boil and pour it onto the egg mixture, whisking continuously. Pour into a saucepan and, whisking continuously, continue cooking over a low heat until a thick egg custard is reached. Remove from the heat and set aside.

3. Place the remaining sugar in a small saucepan with 3 tablespoons water and cook over a high heat until a caramel forms.

4. Remove from the heat and stir in the remaining water. Place back over a very low heat, stirring well so that the water is thoroughly mixed into the caramel. Allow to warm through.

5. Mix ¾ of the caramel into the egg custard. Pour this into the bowl of the ice cream maker and set the machine in motion. *

6. To make the sauce, mix the cream into the remaining ¼ of caramel and stir well.

7. When the ice cream has crystallized, spoon it into a container and keep in the refrigerator until needed. Serve with the caramel sauce poured over.

* If an ice cream maker is not available, pour the caramel-custard mixture into a bowl and place in freezer until part frozen. Remove from the freezer, whisk and refreeze. Whisk thoroughly until smooth, then pour into a covered container and freeze until firm.

TIME: Preparation takes about 15 minutes and 'cooking' time is approximately 15 minutes. Freezing will take between 45 minutes and 1 hour using an ice cream maker – longer if using the freezer method.

SERVING IDEA: Sprinkle over a little chipped dark chocolate.

WATCHPOINT: Take care when adding the extra water to the caramel as it may spatter.

RHUBARB SORBET

A very refreshing sorbet. Serve as a light dessert
after a particularly rich meal.

SERVES 4

350ml/12fl oz water
175g/6oz sugar
450g/1lb rhubarb

1. Peel the rhubarb and cut the stalks into small pieces.

2. Mix together in a saucepan the water, sugar and rhubarb.

3. Bring to the boil and cook for 5 minutes.

4. Blend until smooth with a hand mixer and pour into the bowl of an ice cream maker. Set the machine in motion and remove when the sorbet is crystalized. Spoon into a container and keep in the freezer until needed. *

* If an ice cream maker is not available, part freeze the mixture in a shallow container, break up gently with a fork and then pour into a covered container and freeze until needed.

TIME: Preparation takes about 10 minutes and freezing in the ice cream maker takes approximately 40 minutes.

SERVING IDEA: Serve on a bed of finely sliced rhubarb which has been cooked for 2 minutes in very little water and sweetened to your liking. Allow the sorbet to soften somewhat before serving.

WATCHPOINT: Stop the ice cream maker and spoon the sorbet into a container when it has crystalized. The mixture should be neither too hard nor too soft.

Banana Ice Cream

*A delicious ice cream that is a favourite with children –
for adults, add a spoonful of rum!*

SERVES 4–6

For 1ltr/1¾ pints egg custard
12 egg yolks
100g/4oz sugar
1ltr/1¾ pints milk

225g/½lb peeled banana
Few drops lemon juice

1. Whisk the eggs and sugar together until the mixture pales. Bring the milk to the boil and stir in the egg-sugar mixture. Reduce the heat and continue stirring until the mixture thickens. For this recipe use 250ml/8 fl oz of the egg custard, using the remainder for other flavours of ice cream.

2. Mash the banana with a fork and add a few drops of lemon juice.

3. Add the banana to the egg custard and blend smooth with a hand mixer.

4. Pour into the bowl of an ice cream maker and set in motion. *

5. Spoon into a container and keep in the freezer until needed.

* If an ice cream maker is not available, pour the mixture into a bowl and place in the freezer until part frozen. Remove from the freezer and whisk. Refreeze and whisk thoroughly until smooth. Pour into a covered container and replace in the freezer until required.

TIME: Preparation takes about 30 minutes and freezing time is approximately 40 minutes to 1 hour (longer if preparing in the freezer).

VARIATION: If you wish to use all the egg custard for the Banana Ice Cream, then increase the amount of bananas used to 1kg/2¼ lbs.

WATCHPOINT: It is important to add the lemon juice to the bananas to prevent them from discolouring.

SERVING IDEA: For adults, sprinkle over raisins or sultanas and a tablespoon of rum.

THYME SORBET

Fresh thyme which is still in flower is used to give a very delicate flavour to this sorbet, which is traditionally served between the fish and meat courses.

SERVES 4

500ml/18fl oz water
150g/5oz sugar
4 small sprigs fresh thyme in flower

---

1. Boil together the water and sugar until a reasonably thick syrup is reached – this will take about 15 minutes.

2. Remove from the heat and add the sprigs of thyme. Remove the thyme from the syrup after 2 minutes and drain the syrup through a very fine sieve.

3. Pour the syrup into an ice cream maker and set in motion. *

4. When the sorbet has crystallized spoon into a container and keep in the freezer until needed.

* If an ice cream maker is not available, pour the strained syrup into a shallow container and place in the freezer until partly frozen. Remove from freezer, gently break the mixture up with a fork, then return to the freezer until needed.

TIME: Preparation time is approximately 30 minutes and crystallizing the sorbet takes about 30 minutes to 1 hour in an ice cream maker – longer if using the freezer method.

VARIATION: Use different herbs to flavour this type of sorbet.

APRICOT ICE ROLL

*A delicious combination of sponge and ice cream
makes a perfect end to any meal.*

SERVES 4

Cake Mixture
2 eggs
60g/2oz sugar
60g/2oz flour

Filling and decorating
4 tbsps apricot jam
570ml/1 pint vanilla ice cream
Cream to decorate
Apricots, halved

1. Beat eggs and sugar until light and fluffy. Carefully fold in flour.

2. Turn onto a greased and floured square cake tin and bake in a preheated oven at 220°C/425°F/Gas Mark 7 for about 12 minutes. Turn out onto a clean cloth and leave to cool.

3. Spread sponge with apricot jam and softened ice cream. Roll up using clean cloth. Place in freezer until ice cream is hardened. Decorate with cream and sliced apricots.

TIME: Preparation takes 35 minutes and cooking takes 12 minutes.

AMARENA ICE CREAM

*Amarena is an Italian variety of plum-coloured cherry
that gives this ice cream its heavenly taste.*

SERVES 4

6 egg yolks
100g/4oz sugar
500ml/18fl oz milk
4 tbsps tinned Amarena cherries,
    in their juice, roughly chopped

1. Whisk together the egg yolks and the sugar until the mixture whitens.

2. Bring the milk to the boil and whisk it into the egg mixture.

3. Reduce the heat and whisk continuously until the mixture thickens.

4. Remove from the heat and stir in the chopped Amarena cherries and their juice.

5. Pour into the bowl of an ice cream maker and set in motion. *

6. Spoon into a container once the ice cream has crystallized, and keep in the freezer until needed.

* If an ice cream maker is not available, pour the mixture into a bowl and place in the freezer until partly frozen. Remove bowl from freezer and whisk the mixture. Refreeze, then whisk again thoroughly, and pour into a covered container. Freeze until firm.

TIME: Preparation time is about 30 minutes and freezing time in the machine between 30 minutes and 1 hour – longer if prepared in a freezer.

SERVING IDEA: Chop a few more cherries and sprinkle over the ice cream just before serving.

WATCHPOINT: It is important to whisk rapidly and constantly when the milk is added to the egg mixture, otherwise the eggs will give a curdled look to the mixture.

CHOCOLATE ICE CREAM

A smooth chocolate ice cream made from a rich egg custard sauce.

SERVES 4

6 egg yolks
100g/4oz sugar
500ml/18fl oz milk
60ml/4 tbsps chocolate powder
   (unsweetened)

1. Whisk the egg yolks and sugar together until the mixture whitens.

2. Bring the milk to the boil in a large saucepan.

3. Whisk in the egg mixture, reduce the heat and whisk continuously until the mixture thickens.

4. Once the sauce is thick, remove from the heat and stir in the chocolate powder.

5. Pour the mixture into the bowl of an ice cream maker and set in motion. *

6. Once the ice cream has crystallized it can be spooned into a container and kept in the freezer until needed.

* If an ice cream maker is not available, pour the mixture into a bowl and place in the freezer until mushy. Remove bowl from freezer and whisk the mixture. Refreeze, whisk thoroughly, pour into a covered container and freeze until firm.

TIME: Preparation takes 30 minutes, crystallizing the ice cream, depending on the machine used, will take between 30 minutes and 1 hour – longer if preparing in the freezer.

SERVING IDEA: Serve with chips of white and plain chocolate.

COOK'S TIP: Use plain, unsweetened chocolate powder for this ice cream.

COCONUT SORBET

Naturally sweet coconut milk and dark rum blend lusciously to produce a sorbet rich with the flavours of the Caribbean.

SERVES 4-6

400g/14oz tin coconut milk
90ml/3fl oz mineral water
90ml/3fl oz dark rum
2 egg whites
Liquid sweetner to taste (optional)
2 bananas, thinly sliced and brushed with
    lemon juice and flaked coconut,
    to decorate

1. Mix the coconut milk with the mineral water, rum and liquid sweetner to taste, if required. Pour into a large freezer container and put into the freezer for 1 hour, or until the sides are beginning to freeze.

2. Using a fork, break the frozen coconut mixture up into a thin slush, making sure that there are no large ice crystals left in the mixture. Return to the freezer and continue freezing for a further hour.

3. Remove the coconut mixture from the freezer, and break up as before with a fork to make a thicker slush. Return the mixture to the freezer whilst you whisk the egg whites.

4. Whisk the egg whites until they form soft peaks.

5. Remove the partially frozen coconut mixture from the freezer and make sure that it can be easily stirred.

6. Carefully fold the egg whites into the coconut mixture, mixing lightly but thoroughly to blend evenly.

7. Return the sorbet to the freezer and freeze until completely set.

8. To serve, remove the sorbet from the freezer 10 minutes before it is required and break it up with a fork into large ice crystals. Pile the crystals into serving dishes and decorate with the banana and the flakes of coconut.

TIME: Preparation takes approximately 20 minutes, freezing takes 2-3 hours.

VARIATION: Use pineapple juice in place of the rum, and serve with pineapple pieces and coconut flakes.

PREPARATION: Make sure that the ice crystals are not too wet when you fold in the egg whites, otherwise the mixture will separate during freezing.

COOK'S TIP: Make double quantities of this sorbet, as it freezes well for up to 3 months and is ideal as a stand-by dessert.

MANGO SORBET

*This delicious cool sorbet can be used either as a
dessert, or as a refresher between courses.*

SERVES 4

3 mangoes
Juice of ½ lime
120ml/4fl oz dry white wine
120ml/4fl oz mineral water
1 egg white
Liquid sweetener to taste (optional)

1. Peel the mango and cut away the flesh from around the large centre stone.

2. Put the mango flesh into a liquidiser or food processor, and blend until smooth.

3. In a bowl, mix together the lime juice, wine and mineral water. Add this to the liquidised mango and mix thoroughly.

4. Place the mango purée in a freezer and freeze until just beginning to set around the edges.

5. Break up the ice crystals in the mango mixture using a fork.

6. Whisk the egg white until it is stiff, then fold this carefully and thoroughly into the mango mixture. Sweeten with liquid sweetner to taste, if used.

7. Return the mango mixture to the deep freeze, and freeze until completely set.

8. To serve, remove from the deep freeze 10 minutes before required, then spoon into individual serving dishes.

TIME: Preparation takes about 15 minutes, plus freezing time.

VARIATION: Use any other favourite fruit in place of the mango.

SERVING IDEA: Serve with fresh fruit.

Mocha Ice Cream

This ice cream is both rich and creamy and deserves to be saved as a special treat!

SERVES 6

---

2 tbsps instant coffee granules
60ml/4 tbsps butter
120g/4oz soft brown sugar
60ml/4 tbsps cocoa
75ml/5 tbsps water
380ml/13fl oz evaporated milk, chilled

---

1. Put the coffee, butter, sugar, cocoa and water into a saucepan, and heat gently.

2. Stir the mixture until melted, and bring it to the boil. Cool.

3. Beat the chilled evaporated milk in a bowl, until it is thick and frothy. Mix it into the cooled mixture, beating until it is well blended.

4. Pour the mixture into a freezer container and freeze, uncovered, until slushy. Beat the ice cream well and re-freeze until firm.

TIME: 25 minutes, plus freezing.

STRAWBERRY YOGURT ICE

*Ice cream is usually forbidden on a low calorie diet,
but when prepared with low fat natural yogurt and
fresh fruit, it can provide a welcome treat.*

SERVES 4

225g/8oz fresh strawberries
280ml/½ pint low fat natural yogurt
10ml/2 tsps gelatine
30ml/2 tbsps boiling water
1 egg white
Liquid sweetener to taste
Few fresh strawberries for decoration

1. Remove and discard the green stalks and leaves from the top of the strawberries. Roughly chop the fruit.

2. Place the strawberries in a liquidiser, or food processor, along with the yogurt. Blend until smooth.

3. Sprinkle the gelatine over the boiling water in a small bowl. Stand the bowl in another, and pour in enough boiling water to come halfway up the sides of the dish.

4. Allow the gelatine to stand, without stirring, until it has dissolved and the liquid has cleared.

5. Pour the strawberry mixture into a bowl, and stir in the dissolved gelatine, mixing well to blend evenly. Place the bowl into a deep freeze and chill until just icy around the edges.

6. Remove the bowl from the deep freeze and beat until the chilled mixture is smooth. Return the bowl to the deep freeze and freeze once again in the same way.

7. Remove the bowl from the deep freeze a second time, and whisk with an electric mixer until smooth. Whisk the egg white until it forms soft peaks.

8. Fold the whisked egg white into the partialy set strawberry mixture, carefully lifting and cutting the mixture to keep it light.

9. Sweeten with liquid sweetener to taste, then pour the strawberry ice into a shallow sided ice cream dish, and return to the freezer to freeze until completely set.

10. Remove the ice cream 10 minutes before serving to soften slightly. Pile into serving dishes and decorate with a few extra strawberries.

TIME: Preparation takes about 15 minutes, plus freezing time.

COOK'S TIP: Use frozen or tinned strawberries in place of the fresh strawberries, but drain all the juice away first.

VARIATION: Use any other soft fruit in place of the strawberries. It may be preferable to sieve blackcurrants or raspberries to remove the pips, before adding to the yogurt as a purée.

BRANDY SORBET WITH APPLES AND SULTANAS

Sorbets make an ideal dessert for anyone on a low fat diet.
Try this unusual combination for a real change of flavours.

SERVES 4-6

570ml/1 pint apple juice
60g/2oz caster sugar
45g/1½ oz packet of dried apple flakes
120g/4oz sultanas
140ml/¼ pint brandy
Few drops green food colouring, (optional)
1 egg white

1. Put the apple juice in a heavy-based saucepan along with the sugar. Heat gently, stirring until the sugar has dissolved. Bring the apple juice to the boil and boil quickly for 5 minutes. Remove from the heat and cool completely.

2. Put the apple flakes into a bowl along with the sultanas and brandy. Add enough of the apple syrup to cover the mixture, then allow to soak for 4 hours.

3. Mix the apple flakes, sultanas and brandy together to form a pulp, adding the green colouring at this stage if required.

4. Whisk the apple pulp into the remaining syrup, mixing thoroughly to blend evenly.

5. Pour the apple mixture into a shallow container and freeze for 2 hours or until just beginning to set.

6. Break up the partially frozen ice using a fork or electric whisk, then return to the freezer tray and continue to freeze for another hour.

7. Break up the ice crystals again, but this time mash thoroughly until they form a thick slush.

8. Whisk the egg white until it is stiff, then quickly fold into the ice slush. Return to the freezer tray and freeze until completely solid.

9. Allow the ice to soften for 15 minutes before spooning into individual glass dishes.

TIME: Preparation takes 10 minutes, plus the soaking and freezing time.

COOK'S TIP: Use half a pint of apple purée in place of the apple flakes and reduce the amount of apple juice used to ¾ pint.

VARIATION: Omit the brandy from this recipe and replace with more apple juice.

Index